Using Technology to Engage Students With Learning Disabilities

CORWIN CONNECTED EDUCATORS SERIES

The Edcamp Model: Powering Up Professional Learning
By the Edcamp Foundation @EdcampUSA

Worlds of Making: Best Practices for Establishing a Makerspace for Your School
By Laura Fleming @NMHS_lms

Using Technology to Engage Students With Learning Disabilities
By Billy Krakower @wkrakower and Sharon LePage Plante @iplante

Leading Professional Learning: Tools to Connect and Empower Teachers
By Thomas C. Murray @thomascmurray and Jeffrey Zoul @Jeff_Zoul

*Empowered Schools, Empowered Students: Creating Connected
     and Invested Learners*
By Pernille Ripp @pernilleripp

Blogging for Educators: Writing for Professional Learning
By Starr Sackstein @mssackstein

Principal Professional Development: Leading Learning in the Digital Age
By Joseph Sanfelippo @Joesanfelippofc and Tony Sinanis @TonySinanis

The Power of Branding: Telling Your School's Story
By Tony Sinanis @TonySinanis and Joseph Sanfelippo @Joesanfelippofc

Confident Voices: Digital Tools for Language Acquisition
By John Spencer @spencerideas

The Educator's Guide to Creating Connections
Edited by Tom Whitby @tomwhitby

The Relevant Educator: How Connectedness Empowers Learning
By Tom Whitby @tomwhitby and Steven W. Anderson @web20classroom

Using Technology to Engage Students With Learning Disabilities

Billy Krakower

Sharon LePage Plante

CORWIN
A SAGE Company

FOR INFORMATION:

Corwin

A SAGE Company

2455 Teller Road

Thousand Oaks, California 91320

(800) 233–9936

www.corwin.com

SAGE Publications Ltd.

1 Oliver's Yard

55 City Road

London EC1Y 1SP

United Kingdom

SAGE Publications India Pvt. Ltd.

B 1/I 1 Mohan Cooperative Industrial Area

Mathura Road, New Delhi 110 044

India

SAGE Publications Asia-Pacific Pte. Ltd.

3 Church Street

#10–04 Samsung Hub

Singapore 049483

Library of Congress Cataloging-in-Publication Data

Names: Krakower, Billy, author. | Plante, Sharon LePage, author.

Title: Using technology to engage students with learning disabilities / William Krakower, Sharon LePage Plante.

Description: Thousand Oaks, California : Corwin, A SAGE Company, 2016. | Series: Corwin connected educators series | Includes bibliographical references.

Identifiers: LCCN 2015035347 | ISBN 978-1-5063-1826-4 (pbk.: alk. paper)

Subjects: LCSH: Special education—Technological innovations. | Children with disabilities—Education. | Educational technology.

Classification: LCC LC4024 .K73 2016 | DDC 371.9/0433—dc23 LC record available at http://lccn.loc.gov/2015035347

This book is printed on acid-free paper.

Acquisitions Editor: Ariel Bartlett

Editorial Assistant: Andrew Olson

Production Editor: Amy Schroller

Copy Editor: Jocelyn M. Rau

Typesetter: C&M Digitals (P) Ltd.

Proofreader: Carole Quandt

Cover and Interior Designer: Janet Kiesel

Marketing Manager: Stephanie Trkay

16 17 18 19 20 10 9 8 7 6 5 4 3 2 1

Contents

Preface

My best friend is a high school math teacher. When I started working on the Corwin Connected Educators series, I excitedly told her about the power of using social media to connect with other educators. I passed on what I learned from the authors in this series: that the greatest resource educators have is each other. At a conference, she heard Jennie Magiera speak and finally made the leap to getting on Twitter. Although I wasn't sure she would continue tweeting, she did, and even joined Twitter chats like #connectedtl and #slowmathchat. A few days later, she texted me saying, "I seriously cannot thank you enough. You have changed my life."

Being "connected" seems deceptively simple: Just get on Twitter, right? But that's really not enough. For those who truly embrace connectedness, it's a lifestyle change, an openness to sharing and learning in an entirely new environment. We're seeing the impact of this shift in mindset worldwide. Policies are changing, new jobs in education are being created, hitherto impossible collaborations are happening, pedagogy is evolving, and there's a heightened awareness of each person's individual impact. All of these changes are explored in the Connected Educators series.

While you can see the full list of books on the series page, we're introducing several new books to the series; they will be published in the fall of 2015 and spring of 2016. These books each contribute something unique and necessary not only for educators who are new to the world of connected education, but also for those who have been immersed in it for some time.

Tom Whitby, coauthor of *The Relevant Educator,* has brought together a group of experienced connected educators in his new book, *The Educator's Guide to Creating Connections.* Contributors Pam Moran, George Couros, Kyle Pace, Adam Bellow, Lisa Nielsen, Kristen Swanson, Steven Anderson, and Shannon McClintock Miller discuss the ways that connectedness has impacted them and the benefits it can have for all educators—policy makers, school and district leaders, and teachers.

While all connected educators are evangelists for being connected, connectedness does not necessarily prevent common problems, such as isolation in leadership. In *Breaking Out of Isolation,* Spike Cook, Jessica Johnson, and Theresa Stager explain how connectedness can alleviate the loneliness leaders can feel in their position and also, when used effectively, help leaders maintain balance in their lives and stay motivated.

For districts and schools embracing the connected mindset and empowering all of their learners to use technology, a solid plan for digital citizenship is a must. In *Digital Citizenship,* Susan Bearden provides a look at how leaders can prepare teachers and students for the new responsibilities of using technology and interacting with others on a truly global platform.

Connected education provides unique opportunities for teachers in their classrooms as well. In *Standing in the Gap,* Lisa Dabbs and Nicol R. Howard explore the ways that social media can specifically help new teachers find resources, connect to mentors, and encourage each other in their careers. Erin Klein, Tom Murray, A. J. Juliani, and Ben Gilpin show how teachers can purposefully integrate technology and empower their students in both physical and digital classrooms in *Redesigning Learning Spaces.*

One of the most powerful impacts connected education can have is in reaching marginalized populations. In *Confident Voices,* John Spencer shows how social media and other technology tools can empower English language learners. Billy Krakower and Sharon LePage Plante have also discovered that technology can reach special and gifted learners as well.

The books in the Corwin Connected Educators series are supported by a companion website featuring videos, articles, downloadable forms, and other resources to help you as you start and continue your journey. Best of all, the authors in the series want to connect with *you!* We've provided their Twitter handles and other contact information on the companion website.

Once you've taken the step to joining a network, don't stop there. Share what you're doing; you never know when it will help someone else!

—*Peter DeWitt, Series Editor*
@PeterMDeWitt

—*Ariel Bartlett, Acquisitions Editor*
@arielkbartlett

About the Authors

Billy Krakower (@wkrakower) is a full-time teacher at Woodland Park Public Schools in Woodland Park, New Jersey, where he has taught computers and special education to Grades 3 and 4 for more than eight years. He is the chief financial and event officer for Evolving Educators, LLC (www.evolvingeducators.com). Billy co-moderates two weekly Twitter chats, #NJed chat and #satchat (for educational leaders). He cohosts "SatChat Radio," a weekly show interviewing educators on BAM! Radio Network and available on iTunes. Billy is one of the lead organizers of EdCampNJ and EdCamp Leadership North NJ. He is on the teacher advisory board for ReadWorks. Billy is a 2014 ASCD Emerging Leader, he is a member of the NJASCD Executive Board, and he serves as the Technology Committee Chair. He also served as co-director of NJ-ASCD Northern Region (Fall 2013–June 2015). He has presented at more than 20 local and national technology conferences on topics including Twitter and You, The Science Behind a Mystery Location Call, and Connecting Beyond the Classroom.

Billy has an Advanced Certificate in Educational Leadership and a dual Master's Degree in Special Education and Elementary Education from Long Island University. Billy is a Google Certified Educator and an Edmodo Certified Trainer. You can read more about Billy, his awards, and his presentations at www.billykrakower.com. He is passionate about helping every child and adult enjoy and learn using technology tools in easy, fun, and empowering ways.

Sharon LePage Plante, an educator with more than 19 years teaching experience in special education, has been an educator at Eagle Hill Southport for more than 11 years, as well as currently serving as Director of Technology. She holds a BA in Child Development from Connecticut College, an MEd in Special Education from George Mason University, and a Certificate in Administration and Leadership from Sacred Heart University. Sharon utilizes her educational training and love of technology to engage students with learning disabilities in building their skills and finding success. She has presented at Everyone Reading, EdRev, Edscape, ATIA (Assistive Technology Industry Association), IDA (International Dyslexia Association), and the New York Chapter of ALTA (Academic Language Trainers Association), as well as at several EdCamps, on using technology to empower the dyslexic/LD learner. Sharon is the 2015–2017 chair of the Connecticut Association of Independent Schools Commission on Technology, as well as a member of the Board for Smart Kids with Learning Disabilities. Additionally, she hosts a podcast for BAM! Radio Network called Learning Differently, bringing together the voices of those working with the many aspects of special education and blogs at iplantes.com. Sharon is a cofounder of #edtechchat, a weekly Twitter chat and podcast. She is also the co-organizer of EdCampSWCT and EdCampCAIS.

Introduction

S pecial education is often pushed to the side, yet these students need our support the most. As educators in the field of special education, we believe that this is a very important topic that needs to be covered in the Corwin Connected Educators series. All the new and emerging technologies that are now available for special education can truly impact learner engagement and help level the playing field for special education students. Assistive technologies, such as text-to-speech (TTS) and speech-to-text (STT), have been around for years, but the fact that almost every student now has a device in hand that has these valuable features built in takes away the stigma of utilizing technology in learning. We have collaborated with special education teachers and assistive technology experts to introduce the possibilities that exist for any learner, but most especially for learners with learning disabilities (LD), to capitalize on strengths while supporting weaknesses through the use of the technologies that currently exist in the learning landscape. *(We refer to learning disabilities throughout this book as per the federal definition for Specific Learning Disability as defined in the Appendix.)*

What, How, and Why

LIGHTS, CAMERA,
ACTION . . . HOW WE GOT STARTED

Back in 2014, Sharon and Billy were discussing various ways in which we differentiate with technology and other tools in our classrooms. We both were teaching special education students in a small group setting in Grades 3 and 4. Through this discussion, we decided to develop a technology-based collaborative writing project for our students, since we both had a large number of boys in the class who were the same age. Sharon suggested that we use LEGO's StoryStarter Kit to have the students create a story, as she found it to be highly motivating with her elementary-aged writing students. Being able to motivate students with learning disabilities is important to keep them focused and on track during the day. Not only did the students enjoy it, but we found the LEGO StoryStarter Kit helpful for improving many skills, such as:

- "Literacy skills, including writing, language, and reading comprehension abilities.
- Communication skills, including speaking, listening, and presentation capabilities.
- Collaboration and teamwork skills.
- Digital literacy skills via the unique *StoryVisualizer* software."[1]

Sharon shared how her students loved creating stories using LEGOs, and Billy agreed that this would be a great way to get his students engaged in writing as well. We decided that the students would create stories based on Mo Willems's Pigeon books.

We first introduced the classes, one in Connecticut and one in New Jersey, via a Google Hangout. Students enjoyed seeing and finding out more about each other. We then connected the students via Edmodo, providing clear guidelines for interactions on that platform. The creation ensued, and as the students created their LEGO scenes and stories, we connected them periodically via Google Hangout to check in. The project culminated with stories being shared on Edmodo for students to comment as was appropriate and through a series of Google Hangouts for students to present their creations and explain or tell their stories.

Students came away with not just a broader audience for storytelling but an understanding of how audience plays a role in their writing. Additionally, they realized the connectivity and collaboration that can occur with today's technology. Most importantly of all, they found a multimodal engagement in writing that was beyond words on a page.

IT'S NOT ABOUT THE TECH, BUT FOR SOME STUDENTS IT IS

Technology has infiltrated education in so many different ways, yet one key point consistently reiterated by educators is that,

---

1. Education.lego.com. (2015). *LEGO.com Elementary - StoryStarter*. Retrieved June 7, 2015, from https://education.lego.com/en-us/lesi/elementary/story starter

"It's not about the technology but about the pedagogy." In the inclusion of technology, it is key to focus on the purpose it plays to the end goal of student learning.

In any classroom, technology can be very powerful in class lessons, yet it should only be considered as a tool, similar to other educational tools, that provides a means to an end.

Technology can make it easier for educators to differentiate for diverse learning strengths and weaknesses, particularly under the ideals of Universal Design for Learning (UDL). Even so, this can also be done without technology. So again, it's not about the technology, but about the purpose of and plan for the lesson or skill instruction.

However . . .
          For some students . . .
                    It IS about the tech!

When considering students identified as having a learning disability (LD), technology takes on a whole new focus and importance. It goes from being simply a tool, to becoming the pathway to access content and demonstrate knowledge in ways that provide a scaffolding around the students' learning needs. It is just as important as glasses to see and hearing aids to hear. Today's technology for these LD students becomes the reader, the scribe, and the organizer. What is now everyday technology has the power to be the path to successful learning, not for the end of goal of the lesson, but for its starting point as a way to engage in and understand learning as a whole.

Technology for the LD learner becomes about fostering independence and a successful path to be part of the lesson. LD students need permission to show the power they have within. The tech is just the glasses and hearing aid that their brain needs. When these students grow to be independent learners with the aid of technology, they can then become part of the active lesson alongside their peers. Technology doesn't require them to be pulled out; it doesn't require them to be the one with a dedicated professional as support; it doesn't make the difference stand out. Training them to use the power in these devices puts these learners in the driver's seat of their education.

So yes, the inclusion of technology is just a tool, but consider your learners and for whom this tool can be the starting point to success in our classrooms, not just the means to meeting the lesson purpose.

THOUGHT TO PONDER

Do you know the difference between differentiation and the use of assistive technology? Why does it matter?

The key to addressing learning differences in the classroom is the incorporation of two concepts: differentiation and assistive technology. While closely related, there are some differences. *Assistive technology* is defined as "any item, piece of equipment, or product system, whether acquired commercially off the shelf, modified, or customized, that is used to increase, maintain, or improve the functional capabilities of a child with a disability. The term does not include a medical device that is surgically implanted, or the replacement of such device."[2] These are the tools that are a must for a student to complete a task (i.e., speech-to-text because of dysgraphia or motor issues, text-to-speech due to reading difficulties).

In contrast, "*differentiated instruction* is a process to approach teaching and learning for students of differing abilities in the same class"[3] (i.e, completing a multi-media presentation rather than a five-page report, provide an article in a variety of lexile levels). Differentiation embraces the framework of Universal Design for Learning (UDL) in that it considers all the learners in the classroom, whereas assistive technology may be the tool needed for some learners to access content and demonstrate their knowledge due to their disability. Both aspects are incorporated to

---

2. Atp.ne.gov. (2015). *AT in Education - Definitions & Legal Requirements.* Retrieved February 21, 2015, from http://www.atp.ne.gov/techassist/def-legal.html

3. Hall, T. (2002). *Differentiated instruction* [Online]. Wakefield, MA: CAST. Available from http://www.cast.org/system/galleries/download/ncac/DifInstruc.pdf

address the variability of learners in the classroom. The key is to consider the learners' needs and the level of support that may need to be engaged to provide opportunities for engagement, remediation, and compensation, but mostly for success.

 STOP, DROP, AND REFLECT

What different types of technology do we have access to every day that can help LD students? Consider what capabilities exist in the technology and the tools you are already using. What can you or the student incorporate to make learning more attainable?

Today's tools and technologies are primed to meet the needs of those with learning differences who are struggling in traditional classrooms; however, the lack of awareness and understanding of these tools means they are not being implemented. Special education has reached a wonderful point in that the tools that exist today to differentiate are in everyday technology that students are eager to use. While the tools are readily available, the widespread knowledge of and and how to utilize them is lacking. The range of tools, apps, and websites entering the educational landscape are ever changing, and there are no one-size-fits-all solutions for those with learning disabilities. As with the construct of UDL, differentiation of the implementation of technology to provide assistance in learning is just as key. Throughout the rest of the book, a variety of tools will be introduced and discussed for possible ways to incorporate for LD students; however, the information provided can be applied to any learner. The technologies discussed are by no means the only ones that exist but are examples of ones that represent ways to provide assistance and differentiation in a variety of subject areas. They represent the possibility to provide for LD students the opportunity to find their own academic successes. Additionally, the examples provided are just suggested ways to incorporate technology that we have found beneficial with our learners and within our environments.

CHAPTER
2

Rocking Reading
and Writing

The field of assistive technology has reached a turning point because so many tools are available in the everyday technology that students are eager to use. However, we often find that despite students' enthusiasm, their teachers are often unsure how to maximize these tools for learning. This chapter will outline the built-in accessibility features in many of today's technologies, along with add-ons, for purchase, and web-based tools that exist to support and enhance learning for a range of learners.

Reading and writing are two major areas of education, being the building blocks for accessing and producing information in all academic areas. The tools and technologies that exist to support and differentiate for each of these areas are ever growing.

Today's technologies make providing accessibility to those with learning disabilities so much easier. We can literally put the tools in students' hands and build independence within minutes. No matter the platform or device, the ability to use text-to-speech (TTS) or speech-to-text (STT) is a few settings or app installations away. What's more, the utilization of these tools has become mainstream, thus making usage of the tools less different and more desired.

APPLE, ANDROID, CHROME APPS, AND EXTENSIONS, OH MY!

Built-in accessibility options are a wonderful place to start for many learners before moving to paid programs or apps. For many, the features that come already loaded onto devices will be enough support and provide the greatest ease for buy-in from reluctant users.

Why Eagle Hill Southport Chose iOS as Its Go-To Platform for Their Students With Language-Based Learning Disabilities.

When Sharon's school decided to go one-to-one (meaning one device for every student), the iPad was the immediate go-to due to the readily available built-in accessibility and wide variety of apps. Additionally, the implementation of a Bring Your Own Device program led to the majority of students entering the class-room with iPads that they already owned. This was a great opportunity to add instruction of the accessibility features that Apple continues to hone in its iOS platform. Apple really knocks it out of the park as a user-friendly, student-engaging, assistive device. The series of options and the ease of usage of them has made a marked impact for many users. As noted by Dr. Sally Shaywitz in her book *Overcoming Dyslexia*[1], studies have found that learning disabilities such as dyslexia and dysgraphia are hereditary, and

---

1. Shaywitz, Sally E. (2003). *Overcoming Dyslexia: A New and Complete Science-Based Program for Reading Problems at Any Level*. New York, NY: A.A. Knopf.

the benefits of using these technologies can extend beyond the student to the entire family.

The introduction of the iPhone 4S brought Siri to the subsequent iPhones and iPads (beyond the iPad2). Siri first entertained users with answering questions of all kinds from, "What's the weather?" to "What does the fox say?" Yet it also allowed iOS users to dictate their writing into any app or website. While it isn't always completely accurate and requires the user to be somewhat articulate, it continues to grow and improve through updates. With iOS8, Siri immediately populates the words on the screen as you speak, a key feature students readily embraced. Students often need direct instruction to practice using Siri to dictate their work within word processing apps, as well as for messages and emails or in searches in Safari.

Many features need to be turned on, as they are not natively activated. Users can find these options under Settings—> General—>Accessibility. We will not address all the settings but will discuss a few that stand out for consideration for those with learning disabilities.

1. Invert Colors: This option switches from black text on white to white text on black. This visual difference has been shown to support some with reading difficulties such as dyslexia.

2. Speech: There are a few options under this category to be explored. The first is Speak Selection, which should be turned on immediately. This provides the ability to highlight any text, in any app or website, and have the option to have it read aloud. This can be from a word to an entire page. The rate with which the device reads aloud is set a little farther down that screen with the moving bar under Speaking Rate. When using Speak Selection, the Speaking Rate can only be adjusted from this location. The Voices option only adjusts for languages, not for variations in male versus female or dialects.

FIGURE 2.1 iOS Settings for Accessibility Options

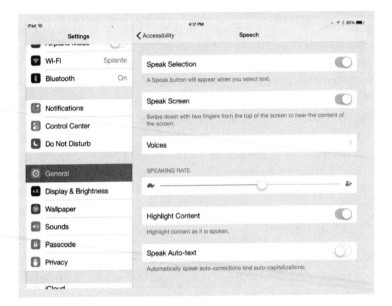

If you can see it, iOS 8 can speak it with Speak Screen. With Speak Selection, the user had to highlight the entire page to have it read, which can be a tedious process at times. With Speak Screen activated, a two-finger swipe down from the top of the screen starts reading right away, with a toolbar appearing to pause, rewind, fast forward, and adjust the speech rate right on the screen you are having read. On the top left of the toolbar is an arrow to minimize and on the top right is an x to quit the option. The one challenge to using this option is that it reads all the text on the screen, which means if one is on a web page, all menus and sidebars will be spoken as well. The way to work around the issue of having all the text of the screen read out loud is to change the view of the web page. When a web page loads in Safari, there are a series of four lines in the left-hand side of the address bar. Selecting those lines will bring the context of the web page forth, eliminating pictures, captions, and extraneous text. This is not available for every web page, but if it is, it makes the use of Speak Screen much more user friendly. In iBooks, Speak Screen magic can also turn any printed book into an audiobook, including automatically moving to the next page.

Farther down in the Speech options is Highlight Content. Activating this option highlights each word as it is read, which can support tracking and visual and auditory support to unfamiliar words. There are many other accessibility options to meet the needs of other disabilities that can be explored.

Can iOS8 read your mind? An additional feature added in iOS8 is word prediction. For any user using the on-screen keyboard, words are predicted as the user types, which can support those with spelling difficulties as well as aid in word choice and retrieval. This is automatically built in and does not need to be activated. It's like the device knows what you are trying to say!

EYES OR EARS: WITH WHICH DO YOU PREFER TO READ?

No matter what subject area of school, reading is required in some shape or form. For those with reading disabilities, this creates a daily challenge, whether it be with decoding and/or comprehension. Providing information in audio format is not novel; books on tape and the Intel Reader have long provided students access to information. However, these also carried the stigma of difference. Today the everyday technology carried in pockets and backpacks can provide support without the shame that often came with using earlier resources. Ben Foss, a successful entrepreneur and inventor of the Intel Reader, who also happens to be dyslexic, even uses an iPhone now to do his reading for him.

Technology Timeout

Karen Janowski—Assistive Technology Stories

In my role as an Assistive and Educational Technology Consultant, I have the opportunity to work with a number of students who struggle with reading and written expression tasks. I was asked to work with a fifth

(Continued)

(Continued)

grade student who desperately wanted to read. She struggled to decode grade level text and told me it took her four months to read one book.

We explored an app called Voice Dream Reader on my iPad. Voice Dream Reader is a reading support app with many customizable features, including customized visual presentation (changes in font, font size, white space, and color choices), highlighted text-to-speech, and customized reading voices and reading rate. We set up the app with the choices Sarah felt worked best for her. Then we enrolled her in Bookshare, a digital text repository of over 350,000 books, which works with Voice Dream Reader. She was allowed to take the iPad home.

One month later, her mother excitedly called to tell me about the success Sarah was experiencing with the iPad. She read FOUR books in one month and for the first time was able to recommend books to her friends. Sarah desperately wanted to read what her friends were reading and participate in conversations about what they read. With the use of technology, she experienced success and independence. She was hooked!

I often receive referrals to work with students who struggle with written expression. It is not unusual for some students to experience "meltdowns" when asked to compose text. This could be due to a variety of reasons: handwriting challenges, difficulty with fine motor tasks, problems with spelling, difficulty organizing ideas, awareness that they are struggling when their peers are not. Chris was one such student. He had great ideas, but he just couldn't get them down on paper. He was in third grade and worked with a 1:1 paraprofessional, as documented in his IEP. One of his accommodations was to dictate to an adult who scribed for him. Fortunately, his 1:1 paraprofessional recognized he was becoming dependent upon her and she hoped there were other options to consider that promoted independence. She asked for an Assistive Technology Consultation.

Together, we explored the use of audio recording tools as an alternative for Chris. Two weeks later, we met again and she reported that Chris quickly learned how to record his thoughts and also used an audio recording tool to take a test independently. The paraprofessional was thrilled because Chris's meltdowns were decreasing in frequency. As Chris experienced success with the use of iPad and computer audio recording tools, he was introduced to the use of word prediction tools, which provided keyboarding and spelling support to promote his ability to word process his work. By the end of the school year, he was writing paragraphs on a computer, independently. Technology made all the difference.

Where's the Material?

Two key resources for families to access books in audio/visual format are Bookshare.org and LearningAlly.org. Both organizations can be utilized by individuals, families, and schools.

Bookshare is free for all qualifying U.S. students. Qualifying individuals who are not students can utilize the service for a minimal fee. Bookshare has over 300,000 titles that are available in digital-voice text format. Books can be read right within Bookshare's free web reader or with a variety of other tools for smartphones, tablets, or computers. Each of the reader tools has various digitized voices and reading features.

Android	iOS	Laptops/Desktops: Windows (W) Macintosh (M)
Go Read Darwin Reader	Voice Dream Reader Read2Go Capti Narrator Kurzweil Firefly K3000	Bookshare Web Reader (W,M) Read:OutLoud Bookshare Edition (W,M) Capti Narrator (W,M) Read and Write Gold (W,M) Kurzweil 1000 & 3000 (W,M)

Learning Ally is a subscription-based service that provides human-narrated books for qualifying persons. Educators may also utilize the service in the classroom. Learning Ally currently has more than 80,000 textbooks and literature books with free apps available for Mac, PC, iOS, and Android devices.

Technology Timeout

Differentiated Reading
Passages With Newsela by Monica Burns

Finding "just-right" reading materials for students can be a challenge in a differentiated classroom. One of my favorite online resources for leveled text is Newsela. With Newsela, teachers can choose an article on a topic in the news. With a few clicks, they can change that article to fit in different Lexile bands—altering the word count, title, captions, and structure.

I'm a big fan of using current events articles as short passages of informational text. It grabs students' attention, connects to the real world, and it piques their curiosity. With Newsela, you can find a compelling news article and tailor it to the needs of your whole class. Students can read a version of the article that is on their level but on the same topic as the rest of their peers. All of your students will engage with the same content but with a text that is at their independent or instructional level.

One thing that I love about this particular site is that each version of the article has a unique web link. That means that I can connect the individual articles to QR codes. I can make a green QR code for one group of readers to scan, a blue QR code for another group, and so on. When I send students off to locate the text that is just right for them, they can scan and access a text to read off of a tablet.

Newsela has become my go-to website when preparing for reading lessons. Whether you are looking for "just-right" resources for your whole class or a small group of students, Newsela is worth checking out. It's free, easy to navigate, and a great site for locating quality informational text.

SHINING WITH CHROME

The landscape of assistive technology in Chrome is ever growing, yet requires installing apps and extensions to build the toolbox. One key feature is that these apps and extensions are tied to the user's Google login, so no matter what device they are on, once installed, apps and extensions follow the user, not the device. Users can find free and paid apps and extensions to fit their needs, and luckily for users, two recognizable assistive technology software companies, *Text Help* and *Don Johnston, Inc*, are competing for recognition as the go-to tools in the Chrome platform, just as they used to in the desktop landscape.

Text Help has brought features of their robust **Read&Write Gold** to Chrome. **Read&Write for Google** is a key tool available, as it works with any textual web page, but it's full-featured version is not free. It provides multimodal access to pdfs, docs, and any online text with TTS and STT, along with a series of other features that can benefit any learner. Word prediction is built into the floating toolbar along with a dictionary, while also including picture dictionary to support younger users.

Gone are the days of color-coded note cards and highlighters with this tool. Users can highlight key points, words, and/or ideas and export them to their own Google Doc. Once in the new document, the highlights are editable so students can rewrite those important details in their own words. Educators who are part of a Google Apps for Education school can get the premium version for free. Student single licenses are $100 per year, or schools can explore a school/district-wide subscription model.

Don Johnston, Inc, introduced **Snap&Read Universal** that is a text reader, text leveler, and can also be a translator. It can easily adjust complex passages for decoding and vocabulary without changing the meanings (working with the robust free tool Rewordify.com), while also tracking data for teachers to see what level students are reading and how much time they spend on articles. **Snap&Read** can work with a variety of platforms including PDFs, Bookshare.org, images, and regular text files and can also work offline. They also have their **Co:Writer Universal** available as an extension. The word prediction is very robust in **Co:Writer**, incorporating the ability to build topical dictionaries that enhance the words being provided to flow with a student's focus. Additionally, **Co:Writer** has automatic speech-to-text for users to continuously be able to assess their writing visually and auditorily.

The challenge with the ever-growing number of options, apps, and sites available is that choosing the "right" tool can be overwhelming. Technology integration and implementation should begin with the LD student's strengths and areas of need in mind. Working with an educator who has an understanding of the tools available can guide this process to be more successful, and for some students, just learning how to use the built-in accessibility features may be enough to support text-to-speech and speech-to-text needs.

Technology Timeout

SpeakIt! Chrome Extension With Natalie Franzi

As a Supervisor of Curriculum and Instruction, I often go into classrooms to consult and work with struggling students. Coming from the special education world, one of my passions is to integrate technology into the classroom to provide equal access for struggling learners.

During one of my consult times, I was working with a boy who was trying to research sea animals. Although the internet sites that were provided were at a first grade reading level, Evan could not access the information. He was frustrated by the task of trying to decode the text and take away the meaning to complete the assignment. I noticed that Evan was adept with using a Chromebook, and we installed the SpeakIt! extension. The SpeakIt! extension converts text to speech and allows for the user to customize the voice and speed.

Evan's face lit up as he listened to how the extension read the text to him by simply highlighting it with his mouse. He played with the voice speed to find a setting that worked best for him. With the installation of this free tool, Evan's reading disability would not stand in the way of accessing grade level texts. We also gave Evan earbuds that he was proud to keep in his desk because it made him feel special to have a tool to which his classmates did not have access. The saying "fair isn't always equal" holds true for students like Evan. He now has the ability to independently access texts on his own that are above his reading level. Evan can now confidently complete research assignments without his reading disability becoming a hurdle.

 STOP, DROP, AND REFLECT

As an educator, do you plan for the lesson or for the learner? It is so easy to get caught up in ensuring content is taught, we don't ask ourselves what, why, and how. Think of the last lesson you taught—in what form was it presented? Why were you teaching it and was that made clear? And did students have a choice in the ways they showed how they connected with the material?

CHAPTER

3

Mastering Mathematics

With the many mathematics concepts covered in elementary through high school, many challenges in comprehension and assignment completion can be encountered by learners with dyscalculia. They may need extra practice and review or tools that help them work through various problems and concepts. This chapter will address tools and technologies for many aspects of mathematics for teacher instruction and student interaction that can benefit all learners.

TECHNOLOGY TOOLS TO ENHANCE LESSONS

Billy does not have a lot of access to iPads or other devices but teaches with a Smartboard and a PC computer. He has found a number of websites to be very useful for students with learning disabilities. These websites were chosen because they allow students to practice arithmetic facts.

There are many websites that can be used to help reinforce basic math skills with which students with learning disabilities can practice. When Billy first started teaching about nine years ago, he decided to curate mathematical websites that he was using with his students. You can find links to these resources on our companion website. Students wanted to be able to use the websites at home to reinforce their learning.

One favorite website for students to practice addition, subtraction, multiplication, and division facts is Multiplication.com. Another favorite of students are the math games on FunBrain.com. Both of these sites are free but do have advertisements on them.

Recently, Billy has been using sumdog.com in his classroom; he allows his students to play for 15 to 20 minutes. What is great about sumdog.com is that Billy can choose the levels and skills he wants his students to practice, and he also gets reports on how his students are doing with their skills. The students can either play one another in class or play against other students around the world.

Common Core and testing online is always difficult for students with learning disabilities. A number of sites are coming out that help prepare students for Partnership for Assessment of Readiness for College and Careers (PARCC) and other online tests. Edcite is easy to navigate and is user friendly. As the teacher, you can also choose the level of difficulty you want for students.

As mentioned in Chapter 2 on reading and writing, there are many built-in accessibility options that are already available to students. Options for text-to-speech (TTS) or speech-to-text (STT) can be just as important to mathematics as they are to reading and writing. Students with learning disabilities often struggle decoding and comprehending word problems. Dyslexic students might have a great grasp on the concept of math, but if they cannot read it, then they are left to struggle.

In working with her math students, Sharon found she often wanted to catch their live process of problem solving. One way to do this is to utilize a screencasting app such as EduCreations or

Explain Everything. She would write a problem up on the white-board, then students would copy it down on the screen of their own device and record their solving of the problem. She could then have students share those with her privately or share via projection to the class. In math, it's not always the answer that is the focus, but the problem-solving methods that need focus for LD students. Explain Everything now holds the added benefit that a teacher can set up problems ahead of time and share the file to students through Google Classroom as an assignment to be completed and submitted.

Apps available on iOS for students for all different grade levels are vast and varied. A few favorites for elementary students are Sushi Monster, Math Ninja, and Monster Math. Fluency in math is very important for students with learning disabilities to achieve. Oftentimes parents ask what their child can do at home to make sure they are practicing their facts, and the variety of engaging, fact-based apps is sure to provide practice while being interesting.

Dyscalculia and dyslexia are not alone in their impact on student engagement in math. For those with dysgraphia, simply having to write about math problems can lead to errors just due to handwriting. Parents of a LD child saw this as an opportunity and created ModMath, an iOS app that allows the student to utilize the touch-screen to set up problems for solving without paper and pencil. This app is designed as graph paper on a device with an in-app keypad to input the problem. ModMath does not solve the problem or incorporate a calculator, putting the computation work on the student while accommodating for handwriting challenges that lead to misaligned problems and computational errors. The solved work can then be emailed to a teacher or to a parent who can print it out. The creators of the app are in the works of building ModMath2 to incorporate feedback from users of the first version.

Note: Parents often ask for recommendations for apps. Graphite .org is a site that has cross-curricular app recommendations for various subject areas and age/grade levels, with authentic user reviews.

Technology Timeout

BrainPOP With Tamera Musiowsky-Borneman

For several years I taught in an Integrated Co-Teaching (ICT) model classroom at the third grade level. The class composition was a 60/40 general to special education population, which included students diagnosed with varying learning or social/emotional disabilities, beginner to intermediate English Language Learners (ELL), and accelerated learners.

To engage all levels of learners, my co-teacher and I used a couple of devices and numerous applications. We used several applications on the iPads, but there were a handful of apps we used very frequently. One of the apps available to students was the Number Pieces app available from Math Learning Center. Sometimes the use of math manipulatives such as base-ten blocks can be more of a hindrance or distraction to a lesson than an enhancement of conceptual learning, so for my very tactile learners, the iPad was available for them to use the virtual base-ten manipulatives. The virtual base-ten blocks were a great tool for students who struggled with the understanding of the base-ten system and place value, and this app allows students to manipulate the base-ten blocks without any pieces falling on the floor.

When students needed additional support on a math topic, they had the opportunity to log in to the BrainPOP app to watch videos on the day's lesson topic. BrainPOP Jr. (grades 2–3) and BrainPOP (grades 4–6) both have vast libraries of videos on math topics, quadrilaterals, or the commutative property of multiplication, as well as other content area topics, that allow students to learn more about a topic in which they need additional support. The stars of the videos are cartoon characters with senses of humor that explain the topic using graphics and examples, and by the end of the video, they have summarized the big idea. Subsequent to the video are quizzes, interactive vocabulary activities, and additional hands-on activities that students can engage in at school or at home.

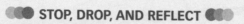

STOP, DROP, AND REFLECT

Math is a great area in which to use various tools to differentiate material and practice. Think of the last math lesson you taught; in what form was it presented? What manipulatives were you using? How were you engaging the students? Did students have choices in the ways they showed how they connected with the material?

Becoming a Study Skills Star

Oftentimes social studies, science, and other subject areas are forgotten or pushed to the side for students with disabilities. Sometimes students with disabilities who are mainstreamed into these subjects struggle because they do not have the direct skill set to apply due to their learning challenges and executive dysfunction. Study skills are important for students to learn and master in these "other" subject areas. Students may need more time or extra review and tools to help them work through various problems and concepts in science. Students should be given note-taking and test-preparation skills in order to help them learn and retain information. Establishing routines will help students develop study skills that will stick with them. This chapter will address tools and technologies for many aspects of the forgotten subject areas for teacher instruction and student interaction that can benefit all learners. Remember, technology is as diverse as children; there is no "one-size-fits-all" solution for study skills.

Technology Timeout

Tools to Differentiate in Projects With Meghan Everette

Technology tools help not only to engage students but also to differentiate instruction when reading, writing, and researching. My first and fourth graders use several simple tools to explore vocabulary.

Students research in the 1:1 iPad environment using a variety of search methods. When studying dinosaurs, students needed to research and write specific facts about what their dinosaur ate, his size, and his appearance. Some students were able to use Discovery Education to search video clips, meaning they didn't have to be able to read well to get the information needed. Other students used KidRex.com to make sure results would be focused and appropriate. Advanced students used "adult" search methods with ease. All students then found images and used ChatterPix to make talking dinosaurs that related their facts. Students with poor spelling and writing skills could make a finished presentation that looked like those of their higher-achieving counterparts.

Educreations, a free creation tool, offers a wide variety of opportunities for my students. One of their favorite activities is taking vocabulary words and finding related images. Students must write or type the word, find an appropriate illustrative image, and write or type a sentence using the word. It is interesting to see students who confidently agreed they knew word meanings in whole group struggle to find appropriate images. Inclusion students use the spell-check feature frequently and typically use very concrete images, while more advanced students compose complex sentences and use abstract or double meanings in their illustrations. Students learn from each other when they watch the final recordings of words and sentences.

ABC Vocabulary is an activity for review that students enjoy. Each student or group tries to identify a word for each letter of the alphabet that works with our topic of study. For example, if we are reviewing grammar terms, students might write A-abbreviation, B-because, C-comma, etc. Students then submit their lists via AirDrop, Google Docs, or using a Neo2 (this exercise works well no matter the platform). I copy and paste the lists into a Wordle or Tagxedo to create a word cloud. The most popular and prevalent terms are repeated and, therefore, larger. Students see many words they could have used but also spend time reviewing and searching text and notes for words that fit each letter. The resulting cloud is not only attractive, it serves as a great study tool that students created themselves.

MAPPING THE MIND

Graphic organizers (also known as mind maps and webs) are not new to the landscape of education. They are staples across many facets of curriculum. They serve great purposes for all learners, yet for students with learning differences, they can be "life or death" for assignments and tests. Graphic organizers lay out information for essays, provide a framework for key details for class and textbook notes, and connect ideas and concepts in a format that can be designed by the learner. Students can master concepts, structure information, and plan out evidence. Keep in mind that direct instruction on how to utilize them effectively is important, just as with any educational tool. Jerry Blumengarten's website, Cybraryman.com, has many great resources for mind mapping. (You can find the link on our companion website.)

Using graphic organizers, the wonder of technology has raised the bar to a multi-sensory level, which is a great bonus to LD learners. These tools can be used for students to take notes in a visual format and organize information in a layout that fits their learning needs. Using electronic graphic organizers gives students choices in formatting the information to meet their needs, unlike the static paper version. Differentiation is in the hands of the student to create with choice. Additionally, students can use typing, word prediction, and/or speech-to-text to input information.

There are a variety of electronic graphic organizers available that can fit students' needs. Some meet the simpler needs of younger or distractible students, while others have more robust features to enable students to create with more customization and creativity.

Getting Inspired With Inspiration

Inspiration Software (Inspiration and Kidspiration) has been around for quite some time and continues to be a poignant tool, if not increasingly so with its addition of iPad apps. Inspiration does need to be purchased for the operating system. Students can manipulate pre-made templates for various subject areas or formulate from scratch, customizing map layouts with color, shapes, and images. Inspiration can be used to map terms and definitions, take chapter notes for study guides, or lay out topical concepts or analyses. Additionally, students can add audio notes to individual

FIGURE 4.1 Inspiration Map

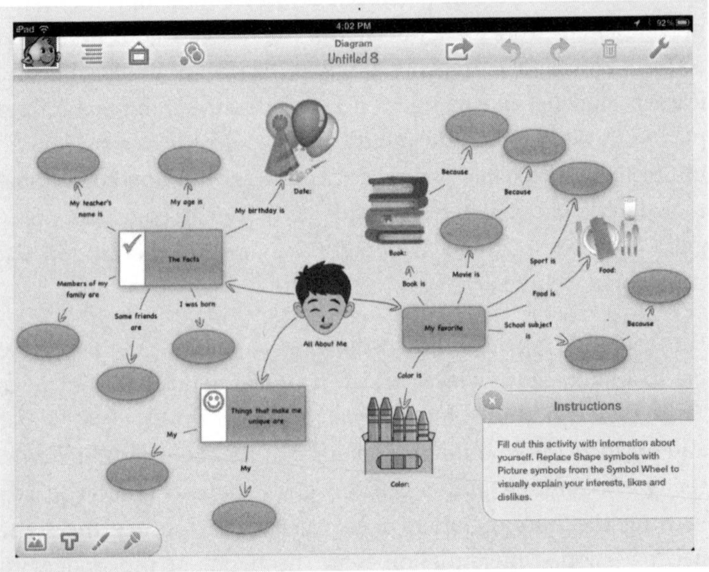

bubbles. Once a web has been created, students can, with the click of an icon, turn it directly into a traditional outline.

FIGURE 4.2 Inspiration Outline

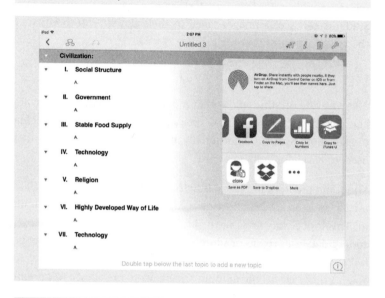

FIGURE 4.3 Kidspiration Outline

Once in that traditional outline format, an Inspiration creation can be exported directly to Pages, where notes can be turned into sentences and paragraphs, saving the student from extra work and making completion of a task flow easier. Inspiration on the iPad has a much more intuitive feel and is easier to manipulate. Students can access images saved to their camera roll to enhance the visual aspect of their diagrams.

Minding Mindomo

A key feature of Mindomo is that it operates and syncs on all available platforms. There is a free version as well as education pricing to gain more features. Additionally, maps can be shared with other users to allow for collaboration.

Mindomo incorporates the ability to attach links and files as well as media, such as images and videos, with search tools for these built in. This tool clearly lays out the layers of information with the user adding details as topics or subtopics. Each layer of subtopics can be hidden temporarily for review practice. An added feature not available in other electronic graphic organizers is the ability to present the mind map as a presentation with zooming features akin to Prezi. This can be beneficial when using Mindomo for a whole class, for student oral reports, or for individual practice with concepts.

Popplet[1]

Popplet is another program for creating graphic organizers and is available on both the iPad and on the Web. It is easy to use and student friendly, and it allows the use of text, images from a picture gallery, or hand-drawn illustrations. Students can use Popplet to record thoughts, take notes, and develop ideas.

Microsoft Word

Microsoft Word has the ability to create circles, squares, or other types of areas in which students can write. Many schools that are

---

1. http://www.techforteachers.net/apps---graphic-organizers.html

Windows-based schools have Microsoft Word already installed on the computers. This is a great tool for students to type their notes or for teachers to create blank sheets for students to take notes. Microsoft products also have speak-to-text features. Students can turn this feature on and be able to dictate their notes as well. See below on how to enable the speak-to-text feature in Microsoft Word.

Add Speak to the Quick Access Toolbar[2]

You can add the Speak command to your Quick Access Toolbar by doing the following:

1. Next to the Quick Access Toolbar, click **Customize Quick Access Toolbar**.

2. Click **More Commands**.

3. In the **Choose commands from** list, select **All Commands**.

4. Scroll down to the **Speak** command, select it, and then click **Add**.

5. Click **OK**.

6. When you want to use the text-to-speech command, click the icon on the Quick Access Toolbar.

Flashcards

Flashcards and repetition are very important to students who have learning disabilities. Students with learning disabilities need to learn to master vocabulary, terminology, and mathematical concepts. There are several different companies that put out flashcard apps.

Quizlet is a great tool that is available on the Web, iPhone, iPad, and Android devices. The description from their website says that "Quizlet's free study tools and apps are used by over a million

---

2. Support.office.com. (2015). *Using the Speak text-to-speech feature.* Retrieved May 10, 2015, from https://support.office.com/en-us/article/Using-the-Speak-text-to-speech-feature-459e7704-a76d-4fe2-ab48-189d6b83333c

students and teachers a day in every country—from grade school to grad school, language learners to vocational students, at home and in the classroom."[3] This is a great tool for all ages. Billy has used Quizlet personally to help study for the Google Educator Exam. Students of all grade levels can use this free tool to help them study; they can also create their own flashcards, putting them into their own words. The ability for students to study from their own device is a great advantage as well, since students today are plugged in 24/7. **Cram** is similar to Quizlet as it is across the Web, iPhone, iPad, and Android devices. It has a large database of preformed vocabulary and allows students to create their own flashcards as well. Both of the companies offer an opportunity for students with learning disabilities to take advantage of studying with flashcards.

Flashcards Deluxe is an app that builds on the incorporation of multisensory learning, as it allows for up to five sides per flashcard. This enables users to not only input words and meanings but add a side for sentences, images, and other inputs to foster engagement with terms. Additionally, it will integrate with Quizlet and utilizes TTS. Students can use the deck in study mode to self-monitor their recall of terms and meanings for future review sessions.

 STOP, DROP, AND REFLECT

Content areas can be the easiest and hardest places to accommodate and differentiate. Besides Google Docs, what are other ways that you encourage students to take notes? What multisensory methods do you use to engage students?

---

3. Quizlet.com. (2015). *For Teachers | Quizlet*. Retrieved May 10, 2015, from https://quizlet.com/teachers

Show What They Know

Creation

O ne of the biggest challenges for LD students is to demonstrate knowledge in a manner that balances their strengths and weaknesses. Allowing students to use tools and technology in a manner that fosters the best output of information provides the teacher with a clearer picture of what concepts are grasped. Traditional papers and exams provide data, but this chapter will outline other ways students can "show what they know" in equally purposeful ways.

Posters, dioramas, and photo collages are wonderful hands-on projects for any learner. They enable students to use visual and kinesthetic skills to demonstrate their comprehension. Incorporating creation tools that are available on devices can enhance multimodal construction of knowledge.

Several years ago, Sharon introduced **Glogster** into her building, and it continues to be a favorite of students and staff. It allows for all-in-one demonstration of knowledge through the use of text, images, and videos, with the design of a poster. The key is to limit the size of space to be used. Students are limited to the space of an 8.5" × 11" piece of paper, yet they can build in multimedia aspects to share their research or information. Through scaffolded rubrics, teachers can differentiate the required elements for the final project while all students are using the same tool.

Adobe Voice became a great addition to the landscape of tools that demonstrate knowledge in non-text-based formats. Similar to VoiceThread, Adobe Voice is a multimedia presentation app that incorporates images or minimal text and, most importantly, the student's voice. Adobe Voice improved this idea with an ease of use and simplicity in execution that makes this tool accessible at any grade level. Students can dictate their information and not have to formulate written information anywhere. This can be a game changer for those with dyslexia, who often rely on tools of dictation for written production, for this makes the visual text not a factor. However, for students with expressive language difficulties, it may not be the best go-to tool without support.

EXPLAIN EVERYTHING

The Uses Are Endless

One tool that continues to take classrooms by storm is **Explain Everything**. One usage was outlined for math in Chapter 3, yet this interactive screencasting, whiteboard-type app has endless possibilities. It can incorporate text, drawings, pictures, video, voice, and so much more.

Sharon uses the Orton-Gillingham approach with her students with language-based learning disabilities. One part of that approach is to have students who are studying roots, prefixes, and suffixes define parts orally as they write them. To do this in a class of five all at once can be a process. Through the use of Explain Everything, she can lay the foundation of the task with oral and visual instructions on one slide while creating the framework for the rest of what the students are to do on the other slides. Through the wonders of the integration ability of Explain Everything with Google Classroom, this lesson could be passed to each student individually for completion, allowing them to record their handwriting and dictation as required, then submitted back for review when each student is finished. At parent-teacher conferencing, the actual student voice and writing recording could be shared with parents as an example of student progress. Additionally, Sharon has used the tool in writing for students to brainstorm writing ideas around an image.

The ability to endlessly develop the usages cross-curricularly with Explain Everything makes it a powerful tool for teacher and student. Teachers can create individualized tasks to share with learners, which can then be completed with the tools that meet each learner's strengths. Students can use various multimodal aspects of the app to demonstrate knowledge, create presentations, or work through problems. Its integration with Google Classroom adds to the power of documenting student work not just anecdotally but with actual student production.

Technology Timeout

Book Creator With Tina Monteleone

Assisting my students with learning disabilities to access the curriculum is my primary function as a special education teacher. Alongside of this comes my responsibility to assist them in finding various ways to express their knowledge and show evidence of learning. With the use of various types of assistive and educational technology, my students have been able to flourish and "show what they know" in ways never originally anticipated. One technological tool, above all, has been a big game changer for me and my students, the iPad.

(Continued)

(Continued)

Over the past few years, I have worked hard to integrate the iPad and apps into my inclusion and resource classrooms. Initially, it was easy to integrate the iPad, especially with my students already coming to me with their knowledge of iOS devices and the use of many different types of apps. Their app activities ranged from gaming, quick photo or video fun, and skill-and-drill apps. Even though I was pleased that they were comfortable with mobiles devices, it did make it very challenging to take my class beyond the skill-and-drill and gaming aspect of iPad use. My students did not view the iPad as a creation tool, but as a "doing" or "entertainment" device. That soon ended with my discovery of the Book Creator app, which managed to open up my view of what an app could do and helped me to show my students the ability of the device as a creation tool.

Book Creator is an amazing app that can give the user the ability to create an interactive digital book. It allows users to create a unit of study or work together to create an authentic part of a curriculum. It has many aspects that make it a highly effective app, including its ability to import media and text, as well as export the final products in multiple formats. This is key because not only does it allow students to create and share content with each other, but it can also allow teachers to have evidence that the students have mastered a content or skill. The other key feature about this app is that it has a simple interface, which allows anyone to begin creating without the need for extensive training.

Initially, I decided to utilize the Book Creator app in our monthly units of science. Since we had been studying the crayfish population that lived in our classroom, the students were highly motivated to expand their learning. This, combined with finding opportunities to bring the ELA Common Core State Standards into science, gave me and my students the opportunity to write and include digital sources in ways unimaginable. With the use of simple rubrics and guidelines, my students were able to take their initial knowledge of crayfish and express their understanding in many ways. Having students express their knowledge in different ways was a key factor for me and my special-needs classroom.

As the projects got underway, my students began importing all kinds of digital media, including pictures, videos, and links to websites that helped to elaborate on the life cycle of the crayfish. Through inquiry and discovery, they were able to search and capture key aspects of the life cycle of the crayfish, as well as being able to identify the functions of each body part. By creating their own unit of study, they were able to explore and understand in a way and depth not originally planned.

With the use of the iPad and the Book Creator app, my reluctant readers and writers have been able to develop a book without even realizing they were reading and writing. They were so engaged in the creation aspect, they did not realize that they were reading, researching, summarizing, analyzing, writing, and applying knowledge that they had obtained independently. They were so proud of what they had created and accomplished that they chose to incorporate a whole presentation piece to the activity. It was so satisfying to see my special-needs students, who typically struggle to express themselves both verbally and nonverbally, present their books to an authentic audience.

 STOP, DROP, AND REFLECT

As an educator, how do you differentiate the ways students show their knowledge? This is not limited to the inclusion of technology but considers how to allow students to use ways beyond the traditional written format to demonstrate their understanding of material or the outcomes of research.

CHAPTER

6

Technology and UDL

U niversal Design for Learning (UDL) is a framework first
defined in the 1990s by David Rose, Ed.D., of the Harvard
School of Education. It addresses the primary understanding that
individuals learn in different ways through multiple means of
engagement, representation, and expression. UDL "is a set of prin-
ciples for curriculum development that give all individuals equal
opportunities to learn. UDL provides a blueprint for creating
instructional goals, methods, materials, and assessments that
work for everyone—not a single, one-size-fits-all solution but
rather flexible approaches that can be customized and adjusted
for individual needs."[1] Creating a learning environment that
embraces these constructs provides opportunity for all learners to
find success.

---

1. National Center on Universal Design for Learning. (n.d.). What IS
Universal Design for Learning? Retrieved February 15, 2015, from http://
www.udlcenter.org/aboutudl/whatisudl

UDL is so much easier to incorporate today through rapidly increasing numbers of tools available to educators and students. Differentiation can be as easy as changing the tool the student uses to engage and demonstrate achievement. Most learning landscapes have opened their doors to a variety of technologies that can be readily leveraged in many ways by the educators or even by the students themselves. Most importantly, for those with learning disabilities(LD), today's tools for differentiation no longer hold the stigma they used to nor highlight disabilities, but provide opportunities to find success in the classroom.

In Universal Design, the "what" of learning speaks to the representation of information learning to comprehension. Varying font styles and sizes, with a variety of spacing, can be a huge difference for LD students. Providing content to be "ear-read" (auditory) as well as "eye-read" (visual) is readily done with today's tech. Using pictures and graphs can build a student's understanding of material while allowing for opportunities of deeper connections with materials. The available software and apps for teachers to put together information in multimodal formats for easy scaffolding are not technology wonders but rather tools that are becoming commonplace. Additionally, the technology can hold the power to provide the assistive or differentiated modality in and of itself. Do you know what your tech can do for you?

As an educator, special or general, we continually consider ways for students to express information and apply knowledge; this is the "how" of learning. Students should be able to express their learning in ways that suit their individual learning style, whether it be video, music, comics, or some other format beyond the traditional 12pt Times New Roman double-spaced assignment. This expands the possibilities for students to produce content in ways that accommodate their learning differences while highlighting areas of strength. UDL "typically involves efforts to expand executive capacity in two ways: 1) by scaffolding lower level skills so that they require less executive processing; and 2) by scaffolding higher level executive skills and strategies so that they are more effective and developed."[2] The tools and technologies existing in not just the classroom but also in students' pockets can provide a host of ways to "show what they know" and the tools needed to externally structure for academic achievement. As educators, so often we dictate what the end products must look like, but what if you set requirements then let the students chose the way to fulfill those requirements?

Finally, the "why" of learning is building and sustaining interest and motivation in learning. Today's technology can make information accessible without the stigma of being different, which is often a huge roadblock to learners. They disengage because they cannot do the same as their peers, and in the past, the methods to make it available were themselves often the reasons why students lose motivation. Providing students with everyday technology that is the same as what everyone else has while allowing the "what" and "how" to work with their learning needs can re-engage students to be active learners. When the material is in a format that they can manipulate, and they can demonstrate their knowledge in formats and modalities that are optimal, students can feel safe to see "why" learning holds relevancy.

 STOP, DROP, AND REFLECT

If UDL has been around for so long, why is it just now making the solid round in educational conversation? Do you know the difference between differentiation and the use of assistive technology? Do you address lessons to the highest, lowest, or middle learner, or better yet to them all?

---

2. National Center on Universal Design for Learning. (n.d.). Principle II. Provide Multiple Means of Action and Expression. Retrieved February 22, 2015, from http://www.udlcenter.org/aboutudl/udlguidelines/principle2#principle2_g5

Conclusion

Addressing the needs of the varied learners that mark every classroom is a challenge for any educator. From a classroom of four to a classroom of 30, each student has their own strengths and weaknesses. For teachers of LD students, addressing learning needs is an ongoing process with no easy answers. The key point to take away is that technologies that are now crossing the thresholds of our schools can be the key tools to addressing the needs of these learners in ways we never could have before. The technology can foster independence at younger ages, can empower the students to capitalize on strengths they may not have easily tapped into before, and can make the task of including them in everyday learning more successful.

There are no one-size-fits-all answers, for all learners are different. Yet we hope this book provides a glimpse into the possibilities that exist for educators, for students, and for families to explore to assist and differentiate so that learning is accessible to all.

For further consideration is how educators interact with their students with content and material. Avenues such as iTunes U and Google Classroom can create active go-to learning spaces for learners that scaffold the process for which they access, interact with, and formulate material. These, along with learning management systems, can provide the needed structure to provide support as students learn to navigate the ebb and flow of their own educational path. The more that can be done to foster independence along with successful learning moments, the more we are doing to help students find their path to value themselves.

Appendix

The Language of Special Education

Special education is a field full of terminology that can be overwhelming to any educator. The need is not to be an expert on the many terms and abbreviations that exist, but rather gain some understanding of them that better equips you to plan for and teach the differentiated student. By no means is this an all-encompassing list, for the field of special education is broad. We include these terms to support your takeaway from the information shared throughout the book. You can help us keep this list current by posting your suggestions and additions to a Google Doc, which you can access via the Corwin Connected Educators Series companion website: www.corwin.com/connectededucators. This chapter presents the language that is associated with working with LD students to give a basic understanding to all those who have found this book to provide the basics of knowledge for using technology for differentiation and assistive support. This list of words, phrases, and abbreviations is in alphabetical order to serve as a quick resource.

504—Section 504 is a federal law designed to protect the rights of individuals with disabilities in programs and activities that receive federal financial assistance from the U.S. Department of Education (ED).[1]

ADHD—Attention Deficit Hyperactivity Disorder. A disability most commonly exhibiting inattention, hyperactivity, and impulsivity, but not all of these need to be present for a child to be diagnosed with ADHD.

---

1. www2.ed.gov. (2015). *Protecting Students With Disabilities*. Retrieved June 14, 2015, from http://www2.ed.gov/about/offices/list/ocr/504faq.html

AT—Assistive technology provides the user the ability to complete tasks that they would not be able to complete without the technology.

Autism—A neurological developmental disorder characterized by significant difficulty with social interactions and communication. It includes symptoms such as poor eye contact, repetitive body movements, and difficulty responding to sensory input.

Differentiation—An approach in which lessons and content are presented in different ways to different groups of students based on learning strengths and weaknesses.

Dyscalculia—A specific learning disability in math where students may have difficulty understanding number-related concepts or using symbols or functions.

Dysgraphia—A specific learning disability in writing where students may have difficulty with legibility and handwriting at age-appropriate speed. Students may also struggle with written expression.

Dyslexia—A specific learning disability in reading where students may have difficulty in reading, spelling, and other print-related tasks.

"Ear-reading"—Ear-reading refers to allowing students to process text through listening versus the traditional eye-reading format in which content is produced. This can be through the use of text-to-speech or audiobook formats.

IEP—Individual Education Plan. Every student who receives special education services is required to have an IEP. The IEP is meant to address specific educational learning goals for the unique learning issues of the student. The IEP is a legally binding document. The school must provide everything it promises in the IEP.

Specific Learning Disability—Federal Definition: *General*. Specific learning disability means a disorder in one or more of the basic psychological processes involved in understanding or in using language, spoken or written, that may manifest itself in an imperfect ability to listen, think, speak, read, write, spell, or to do mathematical calculations, including conditions such as perceptual disabilities, brain injury, minimal brain dysfunction, dyslexia, and developmental aphasia.

(ii) *Disorders not included.* Specific learning disability does not include learning problems that are primarily the result of visual, hearing, or motor disabilities, of mental retardation, of emotional disturbance, or of environmental, cultural, or economic disadvantage.[2]

SPED—Abbreviation for special education.

Speech-to-Text (STT)—STT is the use of one's voice to produce writing, most commonly known as dictation.

Text-to-Speech (TTS)—TTS is the process of having visual text converted to an audio format. This can be completed in a variety of ways using various tools, depending on the original format of the print and available technology.

UDL—Universal Design for Learning is a framework based on research in the learning sciences, including cognitive neuroscience, that guides the development of flexible learning environments that can accommodate individual learning differences.

---

2. http://sped.dpi.wi.gov/sped_ldcriter

Solutions you want. Experts you trust. Results you need.

Author Consulting

AUTHOR CONSULTING

On-site professional learning with sustainable results! Let us help you design a professional learning plan to meet the unique needs of your school or district. www.corwin.com/pd

Institutes

INSTITUTES

Corwin Institutes provide collaborative learning experiences that equip your team with tools and action plans ready for immediate implementation. www.corwin.com/institutes

eCourses

ECOURSES

Practical, flexible online professional learning designed to let you go at your own pace. www.corwin.com/ecourses

Read2Earn

READ2EARN

Did you know you can earn graduate credit for reading this book? Find out how: www.corwin.com/read2earn

Contact an account manager at (800) 831-6640 or visit **www.corwin.com** for more information.

CORWIN
A SAGE Company

Helping educators make the greatest impact

CORWIN HAS ONE MISSION: to enhance education through intentional professional learning.

We build long-term relationships with our authors, educators, clients, and associations who partner with us to develop and continuously improve the best evidence-based practices that establish and support lifelong learning.